TRAVELLERS

GEORGE MACKAY BROWN

TRAVELLERS

POEMS

Edited with an Introduction by
Archie Bevan and Brian Murray

JOHN MURRAY
Albemarle Street, London

Contents

Introduction

'You can't write for three hours every day, six days a week, without having something to show for it!' George Mackay Brown's dedication to his craft and modest recognition of its quality are evident from his reply to a friend's remark on the volume of work he had published, held in reserve, or was presently engaged on less than a week before his death on 13 April 1996. We believe that this latest gathering of some eighty poems is indeed 'something to show'. All but one are printed from unpublished manuscripts or typescripts, or from the newspapers and periodicals in which they appeared. Only 'December Day, Hoy Sound', long out of print and much sought after since *Loaves and Fishes* (1959), is taken from a volume issued by the poet.

Considerations of space and thematic variety resulted in the exclusion of many fine poems from George Mackay Brown's numerous collections. We welcome this opportunity of adding them to the body of his published work. It is also worth noting that well over half the material in this book was produced in the last ten years of the poet's life: an indication that his delight in writing was undiminished.

This book makes available many poems on topics familiar to those who know Brown's work, at the same time as it demonstrates the poet's response to important issues in the modern world. A number of elegies celebrate the lives of figures from history, art and literature, and from Brown's own family and social circle. We encounter Earl Magnus and Earl Rognvald on their way to martyrdom and Jerusalem. Island life is vividly portrayed in lyric and narrative, as are Christ's Nativity and Passion. It is appropriate that the last word is given to the greatest of all the travellers, Ikey Faa, that free spirit of the islands who moves so memorably through George Mackay Brown's poems and stories.

We have no doubt that *Travellers* and its author deserve the recognition given to Mansie, the central character of the opening poem:
'His mouth was a harp. His mouth was a struck harp.'

Archie Bevan
Brian Murray
Autumn 2000

ACKNOWLEDGEMENTS

Several of the poems in this book were first published in one or other of the following: *A Second Scottish Anthology; Birds; Clanjamfrie; First and Always; Glasgow Herald; The Herald; Honour'd Shade; Lines Review; Loaves and Fishes; New Poetry; Phoenix; Poetry Canada Review; Poetry Supplement; Poets and Peasants; The Scotsman; Shorelines; Spectrum; Temenos; Trees; The West Highland Free Press; Zeugma.*

TRAVELLERS

The Green Gate

So Mansie came to the green gate.
A hooded man
Asked Mansie for the password.
Mansie said, 'Password? I came here
Because the road
Stops here (it seems) and I always give a greeting
At an open door, going past.
I have nothing in my hand. I'm sorry.
Seventy years with plough and boat
And never a gift!'
The grave voice said, 'Not a name worth carving in
      marble,
But go in, man. Go in.
Such as it is, you have a story to tell
Different from the memoirs of statesman or poet,
And always
Simplicity is something.'
Mansie went in, clothed with his days
And sat down
At a table with six quiet strangers.
There was food and drink on the board,
From hand to hand a weave of good courtesy
On a loom of silence.
Then a child said to Mansie,
'The face of the man at the gate,
I saw it,
And it was brighter than the sun.'
Their tongues were unlocked at the table then.

Far into the night
They told, one after another, their stories:
Pure as root or shell or star.
Listening, Mansie considered
His days of clay and sweat and sea-slime,
And he shook his head.
But when he stood by the fire at last
His mouth was a harp. His mouth was a struck harp.

1985

Edwin Muir

The labyrinth: an old blind man in the centre of it with a
    crystal key.
The labyrinth: towers, vennels, cellars.
The labyrinth: a wilderness of dark doors, with one bright
    lintel here and there.
  Bright lock by bright lock he turns the crystal key.
At every door, a rag of time falls from him.
  Through ghetto, shambles, graveyard he goes.
  The brightness spills out, spills out before him.
  He brings the poem to the hidden bestiary.
The labyrinth. The labyrinth.
He stands, a young man, at a threshold of unbearable
    brightness.

                              *

The child plays, in his island, his eyes filled with the sun.
Far back, the beast lies in a pool of darkness.
The child goes among the sun-bright ruined stones of the
    labyrinth.
  (The epic is over. The lyrical echoes have not yet
    begun.)
A little ship sails its horizon forever, freighted with bales
    and barrels of the sun.
Below, his father opens the door of a simple field to the
    golden guest, the sun.

                                                May 1979

Modigliani: The Little Peasant

What's he thinking of, sitting there?
He's thinking of a girl,
She who makes cheese and butter in the next farm.

I think he's waiting for the horsemen
To come from the stables.
They're to take him for a pint or two at the inn.

Is he remembering the circus
That passed through, in April,
An elephant, clowns, a drummer?

I think he's been cutting barley all day.
His eyes are sore
With sun, scythe-flashings, corn dust.
Tomorrow, the setting up of stooks.

No: when (he wonders)
Will the farmer's wife call him indoors
For broth and bread?
His nostrils are stretched with kitchen smells.

We stand before him in the gallery now,
Thousands of ghosts.
The Little Peasant welcomes us from the country of
    forever.

Tolstoy

He sits at an oak desk,
    The old lordly peasant,
There is fire about his heart.
In the crucible of his heart
    The ore is troubled.

He swings a scythe,
    In a field, with serfs,
Count Leo Tolstoy,
    In the sweat of his brow
    He scatters the gold of a summer.

He is home from the wars,
    Sword over hearthstone set.
Now the greatest war
Is there for a transmutation (this alchemy?)
    Bald Hills, Natasha, Borodino.

Truth is a clear star.
    Men root among husks and roots.
Clear and simple, the star.
    Tolstoy lay on the rack of age,
The star on his forehead.

The heroes of history
    Perish in their fires,
        Caesar, Napoleon, Genghis Khan.

Time, a wind, mingles their dust
With dust of falcons and flowers.

Look, the crucible is cold,
Look, the manuscript
   Sifts pages across the great oak table,
The sheaves are in the barn.
A book is heavy with jewels and icons.

Spring Equinox 1994

Norman MacCaig

Milne's Bar, Rose Street, Edinburgh –
A Saturday afternoon in 1956.

Sitting here and there about the unlovely tables,
Sydney Goodsir Smith, Tom Scott, Norman MacCaig,
   Robert Garioch, George Campbell Hay, Alexander Scott
And other bards
Whose lyrics, scratched on the backs of envelopes,
Would never fly into books.

A cry on the steps, 'Chris, he's here!'
And the bards rise to greet their king, Hugh MacDiarmid,
Just off the Biggar bus.

(This Orkney bard sits alone.
   He is too shy – as yet – to visit the bards' table.
Enough to look at them, with longing.
Their words have flown out of books
   To sit, singing, on the branches of his blood.)

And now, a few days since,
The last of those poets is dead,
MacCaig, he with the head of a Gaelic chieftain
And the courtesy,
His tongue an edged and glittering dirk
Against whatever is ill made, unworthy.

May the mountains
Gather about him now, in peace, always.

January 1996

Old Woman

None has seen tears from this face
But the mother
And a sharp-tongued teacher
And one ploughman
And a young sea widow
And my bairn in the cradle

But for rain and spindrift
A worn dry stone.

3 August 1987

Elegy for a Child

This second door stood open only a short while.
Now close it gently.
The ghost has gathered its few belongings into a bag.
It has gone through the garden gate.
It has turned its back on the fire, the roses, the stories.

Fragrance from lintel and threshold –
Fragrance of bread –
Fragrance of sharing, after a good word uttered –
Fragrance of laughter too young for mockery.

Have you seen a disturbance in the blue wind
Between the cold hearth and the moor?
The brief flesh
About the bone, brighter than a cornfield
And the ghost beyond dew and snowflakes bright.

(For a short time it is lost – it weeps –
It does not know where to go.
Ears are too gross for its grief and questionings.)

Shut the door gently upon women's weeping.
Twelve hands
Light him in at the door of his first mother.

February 1983 – August 1984

In Memoriam John L. Broom
28 July 1992

*John Broom, an old friend of the poet, was a librarian by
profession, also a Unitarian minister, film buff, and biographer of
John MacLean, the Clydeside socialist.*

In sorrow the bread and salt are eaten.
From first cry to last sinking under wounds like a hunted
     beast,
The circuit is sorrowful.
The man who owns veins of gold
No different from the eater of crusts.

The feast and the dance
Are more beautiful
For that road of thorns and stones.

Somewhere, to all men and women
The summons is coming to a feast, with music and the
     only bread and wine.
  – It is a furrow you follow.

Yesterday we gave the dust of a friend to the wind.
And afterwards
Between a black cliff and the sea
A rosebush was planted.

1992

10

Mhari

Mhari Brown (1891–1967) was the poet's mother.

1

'Go down. Good fishing (lobster, haddock)
   Off Strathy, in the salt streams.
You starve here, in these glens.
   Factor, minister, will speak to those with boat-wit
   In Durness, Scrabster, Wick . . .'

They had not seen sea before.
   To the bleak rocks they came,
Vassals of an English duke.

In hovels above the rocks, starved a summer
Till son and nephew got a measure of sea-wit
   Struggling in skinflint drowning tides.

There, sixth of nine children,
   Mhari spoke the ancient Gaelic
   Till the English schoolmaster came
   To cleanse their tongues of that music.

2

Look: a boy of that clan on the sea-edge
Has prospered in Wick,
   Climbed from 'boots' to own hotels
In Orkney, Caithness, Shetland;
Forgets not his blood,

11

The Sutherland croft lass, and others.
    Mhari, there she is, gray-faced from the Firth
On the *Ola* gangway,
    A parcel of belongings in her Celtic hand.
The gruff hotel-boss: he stands,
Look, with strict impatient hands
    In the door of his big new hotel.

3

Fiddles, melodion, a Town Hall dance,
    Fishermen, country boys, clerks.
Is this sinful?
Is cleaning hotel-rooms on Sabbath sinful?
    The Free Presbyterian rock
    Keeps ancient springs of laughter

And she laughs with the joky postman
    (Waxed moustache, stylised wit)

And round they circle, this time a waltz.

But a kiss, under the streetlamp?
    Sinful, dangerous. 'I won't
    Walk out with that man again . . .'

4

Midsummer. The wedding feast –
    Cheese, lobster, cake, whisky
    In Strathy, small scatter of Celtic crofts.

Tinkers came through the dusk,
    One had a fiddle.
    The parish danced till dawn.

The bridegroom, he was drowning
   In a sea of lovely Gaelic;
And woke, his mouth cold
With dew of the wild white rose.

5

Gentleness, poverty, six children
   (One died) in stone houses
Along Hamnavoe, at close and pier.

A cupboard sparse but never empty,
Oatcakes and bannocks on a smoking griddle,
   The Monday washing
Flaunting, damp flags, in a walled garden,

The paraffin lamp on the winter table,

Jar of bluebells on a sun-touched sill,

And a wordless song moving
   Through the house, upstairs, downstairs,

At the creeled pier, in the bee-thronged garden.

She thanked, out of an ancient courtesy,
   All visitors for calling.

6

No woman but lips many times
   The dark chalice,
Parents, husband, children, friends.

13

A comely sorrow, the mouth tranquil:
Thy will be done.

The first dark petal fell,
Then others, a cluster of shadows,
   Flower of oblivion
   About her gentle turning away.

7

On a winter night, from the Hamnavoe God-acre,
   There, the Strathy Light!
Between, rampant hooves and manes,
   The Pentland Firth.
   The dead lie, rank on rank,
   Facing the sunrise.

Wintered roots coil
   For upsurge, the arms of a girl
   Overbrimming, the new light.

Today, June the fourth, 1993
Mhari – her death month November –
   Had been one hundred and two.

                                   4 June 1993

St Magnus Day 1992

Outside my window daffodils
Dance in the north wind.
In another garden
A blackbird
Clothes, before leaves, a tree in song.

It is Saint Magnus Day.

But for that company of heroes
But for those
Whose blood purified the roots and sources
The daffodils
Would be a measurable disturbance of earth and air today,
That blackbird
A graph on a cold grid of sound.

But the poor still dance (thank God).
Because of the saints
We, a throng out of winter,
Dance now in coats brighter than Solomon.

16 April 1992

Saint Magnus Day

'She's making for the open ocean, that ship,
A scatter of oars
Between here and Rousay.'

'Them and their axes and loot.
This ox, Sam,
He won't have the yoke put on him.
He was awkward last year too.
More of this, Mister Ox,
You'll be pies on the hearth, next winter.'

'What's the priest doing down at the shore?
And that flock of hens, the women?'

'I took that many stones out of the heather
I could build a hut.
Only the laird would charge a rent for such a wilderness.
I tell you this, men,
We're going to have some wrestle with the new ground.'

'Stand still, you brute! Look
At this plough.
More than one spider's wintered here.
Look, a rat's tooth in the share.'

'I told that woman to be here with the ale-skin.
Look, Ragna, says I,
We begin the ploughing at noon.

And there she is, the slut,
Gawping at a longship going past.'

'I don't see shields along the hull.'

'What we need is new strong ploughs,
Curves of Scottish oak.
Then the laird might get his rent on time
If he gave us strong wood
And had less tapestries and goblets
On shipboard, from Dublin, for his lady in Rousay.'

'The candles are lighted in the kirk.
Is there a death in some house?'

'The ship, she's nudging the tide,
Egilsay-bound.
That's it, the bishop's on board.
Oh, how they'll smirk
And curtsy and hand-kiss, our women, soon.'

'All I know is, if we don't put ploughs to the hill
There'll be no bread in winter,
Not a jug of hot ale
When we come in with blue hands from the lobsters.'

'No harvest home. No fiddle, no dancing.'

'Look at that hawk
Up near the sun, slewed north.
A big wind

And he hasn't stirred for eight gatherings
And shatterings of sea.'

'Up, Sam. Up, ox. Kick him.
Sam, you should be glad.
You've been in that dungeon of a byre all winter.
Sun and sweet grass now, Sam.
Sam, think of cornstalks.'

'Simon, you have the thickest shoulders,
Pick up the plough.'

'A man has left the ship.
Look! A man in the sea, his mouth brimming.'
16 April 1988

The Doors of Death

The earl rode past my door, the saddle
  Studded garnet and gold.
The gravedigger held a skull. Ploughmen
Struck the glebe into furrows.

A pilgrim passed my door. He held
  A silver fare in his fingers.
Last ice along the ditches.

A poor man passed my door. He wore
  The mask of man's hunger.

  I am Death. No hearth in my house.

  A poor man sat at my board.
He broke the bread into blessings.

  A pilgrim stood at my thwart. Prow-
Shape, dove-shape, share. A wave
  Traversed him, silvering.

  Who takes plough to the lord's glebe?
Lord or labourer,
  It is man sets out on the long road
  To the Inn of the Cornstalk.

11 April 1992

Earl Rognvald Kolson of Orkney to an Itinerant Builder of Churches

To Master Roger at Durham, builder of kirks,
   It is no clerk or scrivener
      Seals this letter. I am an earl,
Commander of ships, poet,

A man skilled at ordering sounds and silences
   On a winter harp. I pull in nets
      With my fishermen, I delight
In smithy flames, hammerings, hot iron.

All good labour – plough and oar and peat bank – dances
   To original music. I urge now
      A famous maker of stone poems
To meet me in a place of silence.

I say to a skipper, 'Take this letter
   To King Olaf in Norway,
      Unfurl a sail, be swift and sure
As a dove through spindrift.'

And he stows the sealed parchment
   In a leather bag, old shipman,
      Against salt encrustings . . .
Maker of scattered stone ships,

I do not know where skipper or horseman
   Will find you, you and your workmen

Are forever on the roads
Going with your carts, scaffoldings,

Plummets, compasses, ladders, wedges,
    Mortar-boards, hammers, chisels
        (No rest till all get thrown,
Worn out, on the far shore of time).

You do not build town houses
    For merchants, however much gold
        They ring on your bench,
Nor barns, nor lodges, battlements,

But kirks only, *Ad Majorem Dei Gloriam*.
    This morning a thing was told me,
        You and your carts are encamped
About a stone hull in Durham.

A great kirk for the bishop there
    Soars as high as the rooks, I hear.
        The last stone will be locked in
Before the wrecking storms of Yule.

Shipwright in stone, I have purchased
    Three acres of land near Kirkvoe,
        A village in the Orcades
And I've had it long in my mind –

Rather, an angel winged in with it –
    To build a red minster there
        In memory of a murdered uncle.
What! I can hear you growl,

Earl or beggar, this man is a fool –
  I am not a carver of tombstones.
      But if I say, this murdered one
Is Saint Magnus the Martyr

By whose broken skull blind men
    Behold the sweetness of sun again,
        Cripples and mourners dance
To poetry,

And I that whirled away youth
    At ski-slope, tavern, tilt-yard
        Stand in a place of silence.
(The honeycomb is in the rotting lion.)

I have a headland of lavish sandstone.
    In a tall pillar red as fire
        Set the skull, our saint,
Magnus who orders the seven unruly crewmen.

In my smithy, I will beat out
    My blood-crusted axe, to shine
        Candlestick and cruet in our kirk,
My net will hang at the wall.

I desire an ark to carry this people
    To Golden Jerusalem (I am to sail there soon
        In a fleet of fifteen ships,
A frail flutter of poems).

Sir, you will be paid in good Rhenish gold.
    Be at the port of Leith in Scotland

On the Saint's day, mid-April.
Three ships, ample-holded,

Will carry your score of masons,
   Your gear (flutes, chessboards, tankards too)
      All things apt and needful
To build this great red psalm in the islands.

August 1995

23

St Rognvald's Journey to Jerusalem

Rognvald's epic voyage was the inspiration for a major artistic event in the 1993 St Magnus Festival. Fourteen sails painted by local artists were hung in the nave of St Magnus Cathedral. Drawing their inspiration from the poet's laconic text, each of the sails celebrated a 'station' on the great Viking pilgrimage to Jerusalem. This artistic enterprise has now acquired a musical dimension in a sequence of orchestral and choral works composed by Sir Peter Maxwell Davies for the BBC Philharmonic Orchestra.

    I Fifteen keels laid in Norway for Jerusalem-farers

   II In Kirkwall, the first red Saint Magnus stones

  III An Orkney wintering. Stone poems in Orkahowe: 'great treasure . . .'

  IV Bishop William: a blessing on the pilgrim sails

   V Westerly gale in Biscay, salt in the bread broken

  VI The bishop's ship a small storm-tossed kirk

 VII Rognvald and Ermengarde: roses, lyrics in Narbonne

VIII The winter burning of a Spanish castle

  IX Eindred's desertion, five sails dwindling eastward

   X A dromond taken, the torrent of molten gold

  XI Thorbjorn Black, poet, dead under sun-bright stones

 XII Palm branches in Jerusalem: *via crucis*

XIII Byzantium, golden city: the ships and the domes

XIV The return: drying sails in the lofts of St Magnus

3 May 1993

Saint Magnus Day: The Relics

The cleft skull of the martyred St Magnus was discovered in one of the central piers of the cathedral during a major restoration in 1919.

    Bishop William the Old was the first Bishop of Orkney, and occupied the bishopric for well over 50 years.

The standards – Andrew, Columba, Olaf –
Flutter
Like great seabirds outside the door of the kirk.

The torches cluster that were invisible flames
Out in the wind and sun,
Red now inside the cave of the kirk,
One by one, a torch in a socket
Under the branching arches,
A torch for the altar,
A torch for the great pier,
Laved in its own red light,
All but the one
Red stone of burial.

Is that music? Listen, listen.
The jargon
Is far off still between
Peerie Sea and Cornslip,
Fiddles, pipes, a drum,
The beat of ocean in it,
And louder (listen!)

And here in the kirk the harp stands,
A silent angel, waiting
For a meshing of the sea music.

Open the door wide. Open
The west door.
Lights of April – lagoon and lift – light, lap
The feet of the bishop.
But now, red light of stone, torches, tapers.
He comes, Gulielmus Episcopus,
'A clerk of Paris',
And Eynhallow with him, the abbot
And canons and deacons
And last
The little old priest of Egilsay,
He that was in his kirk
That night of cold vigil.
What does the bishop carry
Besides his crozier?
An oaken box with an intricate cleft bone.
See, they process
In gold, scarlet, ivory, jet
To the high altar.
A young monk drifts to the harp. He sits. He waits.

A tumult outside. Listen.
Who makes riot on such a day?
Last scars of snow
Silver are on the hill. Scars
Of fire are on a hill.
They acclaim the death of winter:
Per the fisherman and his crew,

Ikey from the tinker quarry,
Skaf that sweeps leaf and shell from the street,
Vik who cargoes a ship among the islands,
Skald who thongs planks
    above curving
    keel, curve on
    rising curve, and
    caulks and tars,
Bluenose the taverner, Swart the smith,
Sigg of the milk and butter
And men from under the cliff.
Why can the town not come in?
They make a clamour at the mercat cross.
The doorkeeper offers a sign.
They rush, shoulder, stumble, grumble,
Then all ingathered, doucely folded.

The white hood stoops to the harp
Like a swan to a loch.

276 Broomhill Road, Aberdeen
St Magnus Day 1990

The Harp in the Glebe

This poem was specially commissioned to celebrate the residency in Orkney of the Scottish National Youth Orchestra in 1989.

1

Then, after longships, torch and axe,
The skirmish in shore waves, scattering
   Of broch-stones, came a month
   Of hunger, hardship, the yoke

2

On the stubborn ox, a stumbling
On stony furrows, seed-cast, harrows,
   Charting of perilous salt for
   Lobster and ling, long

3

Moor cuttings that a hearthflame
Fail not in the fall and fell of winter.
   Then, the tilth greening,
   Links littered with lambs,

4

Hearthstone and threshold set sure,
The earl spoke. 'Now this steading
   Requires the seal of song,
   A concord of pipes and strings

That the rooting of this folk in Orkney
Be at one with the star streams.'
   That night in the long hall
    Young hands, young mouths, beseeched
    Earth-ore, sun-gold, the cornstalk.

17 March 1989

Earl Rognvald Kolson to An Iceland Poet: AD 1150

Come in September. Then is harp
   Loosed from cobwebs at the wall,
   It rejoices among fires and ice.

Come in September. You will know soon
   Have you come to a hospitable house
   Or will it be thin ale in snow-time.

The poets here will curl their lips.
   They know this, the best bards
   Sail to me from Iceland in September.

Thorbjorn, I will have an ale-mug
   Struck for you. A new lamp,
   In September, beside your scrolls.

Here, in September, over stubble,
   Burnished hand clasps bone hand.
   That treaty, we know, is poetry.

Thorbjorn, you will have sea salt
   In September, on beard and harp.
   And you will be tired of fish.

Inga, that girl, will bring you brightness,
   Sweet well water. Helga,
   In September, will break you a gold crust.

7 September 1995

30

Autumn Cruise

Rolf left stream for streams.
The miller grinds salt.

Sven set foot on a rock, he's
Crabs, cold shells.

Arn's eye
Would have cherished the pure flight and cry of
    the bird that quenched it.

Wolf stooped under a lintel.
There is a lower stone.

Thord? We keep silence.
Thord was soon out of the story.

Aud, silver seeker,
Ten weeks till the snow, Aud.

'Sea sluts, Gerd,
Unravel your Thord . . .'

The ship lies, furled, off More.
Of twenty, seven dry cold oars.

1985

31

The First Castle: Edinburgh

Set up tents on the slope of this crag, twigs and skins.
    Leave the wounded with wolves, far back.
        'Rain in the south? Or dust of hooves?'
        'There are springs of cold sweet water. Dig deep.'
        'Dig deeper till iron rings on stone.'

They make of stones a small sun prison, a smithy.
    (Barns must wait, the smithy comes first.)
    They build first, a keep on the crag, a stone eagle.
    In old words our story has been uttered, in secret, to the
        strong stones.
    They build a house for the daughters of the chief.
        'Make swords, blacksmith, strokes of winter sun.'
    Quarrymen labour at first dawn.
    The masons square stones at sunset, still.
    The women pluck wool, they spin a thin line from the
        fog of wool, they sit at wooden frames inside a tent.
    The young men live in the fortress, in the sign of the
        eagle, high.
Three or four have gone laughing into the forest. Three
        drag a blood-snortled boar. 'Girls, go with oil and
        leaves to the wounded hunter.'

A mule brought baskets of shifting silver,
    Fishermen stood at the loch under the crag.
        Protect us from the Saxons . . .
        Horsemen broke our keels at a shore in the west . . .

Forge roars, a beast in darkness. The rock reels with black
    music.
  The eagle has iron beak and claws.
  A known tribe then, driving swine and cattle north.
      'We will give you this cow of a hundred
              cheeses for hanks of that wool.'
      Why are you hurrying north?

(They urge pig and ox to the shore of the firth, going
    north.)
Girls dance to a swart music. The anvil utters bits of
    strong sun. The eagle will overshadow the Saxons.
The eagle will tear horse from horseman.
Girls and warriors turn about the black sun, a
Celtic wheel. Ice hung gray nails from the stone lintels.

The horsemen came at the time of the first dropped lambs.
  Sunbursts, they blinded a winter folk. A tempest of
  ordered hooves scattered fog and dances, the high
  watcher, the loom and the sweet lost cries of children.
  Bright edges strewed the stones of the keep about the
  high rock. Then was the eagle up in the west. They
  gathered lissom girls to the strong backs of horses.
  They rode with songs into the green sun.

c. *1985*

Gallowsha (A Witch Fire)

Gallowsha was the place of public execution in Kirkwall.

Three Old Women
  Bring in fire! three old women cried.
  Give her the yellow and red coat! But
  no torches were lit before the throat was girdled.

Neighbour
  Was as bonny a bairn as ever wore daisies, she.
  What worm comes in at the mouth, when innocence
  sleeps? It breeds in the heart.

The Stranger
  Oh yes, but she cried. She skirled when she saw
  the post and the rope! She stopped then. She went
  to the hangman laughing like to a lover.

Preacher
  Repent ye, therefore, and turn. Behold the tree of
  sinners, that the rose petals thereof wither like snow,
  and are thorns and ashes soon.

Alewife
  Ale, penny a pot. Cool the flame the poor girl stands
  in. Usque, twopence the glass. Warm a cold spirit.
  It passes.

A Palace Servant

He tried her this way and that last winter, all smiles
and sovereigns, then threatenings. She would not
wait under the moon, burning. Then three strangers
with paper and seal stood at her father's door.

Child

What's that black mask? What gray thing is shaking
under the rope? Mother, why seven torches, and the
sun so bright?

July 1977

Emigrants: 1886

They stood there, in a small flock
At the wooden jetty in Hamnavoe,
Till the gang-plank was let down.
The heart of the small steamer began to beat
And ropes were cast off.
A few stood above, leaning on the rail –
One shepherd smoked his pipe –
All looking at the granite hill
And Hamnavoe, that cluster of stone houses.
The children
Swirled here and there on the deck like happy birds.
Most of the women were below.
They didn't speak. They looked at nothing.

*

As the great ship out of Southampton
Bore them and hundreds of others (strangers)
Round the Cape, and out
Into the Indian Ocean (such warmth and glitter!)
More deeply the new-sharpened chisels
Scored the stone of their minds with last images:
Fishing boats, seals on a skerry,
Peat hills, kestrels, the great plough-horses,
Kirk and tinker-fire and the hard hewn flame
Of St Magnus at sunset –
Rackwick, the green jar tilted at the sea.

Now here, at night, a new star wheel
Rose from the east, slowly and bound them to it.

*

For days Australia filled their horizon.
Strange birds followed the ship.
The children forgot. Their minds
Were scribbled over and again with new scenes.
But the hammer-strokes of their childhood
Cut the men and women to the heart.
And they made their hearts stone
And their lips were like stone,
As the pulse and wash of the ship drove them on.

*

A sailor pointed eastward, 'New Zealand!'
And they saw a snow mountain, far off.
The children stood for a minute,
Their faces all one way: and soon
They were clowns, dancers, disturbers of the peace!
One girl from Hoy looked west and north –
Bird-high her glance, the sun
Glittered across the prisms of her eyes.
But ancient eyes of Celtic stone
Cut through the roots
Of Himalayas, Caucasus, Atlas, Grampians,
And the curving unquiet crystals of two oceans
To a round blue hill, and seals, and a barleyfield.

November 1986

Haiku: for The Holy Places

Orc

Orkney – 'orcs' – the school of sleeping whales,
To those who glimpsed it first,
Hills half-sunk in the sea.

Midsummer

Midsummer, the hills wear fertile patches,
Corn and pasture and meadow,
Long green coats from the hills' throat to the shore.

The Northern Sky

Orkney turns upon poles of light and darkness.
A summer midnight, the north
Is red with the two lamps of dawn and sunset.

Kirkyard

Always, by the shore, kirk and kirkyard.
The legends of the dead, their carved names
Faced east, into first light, among sea sounds.

Wind

Wind always, the unseen summer crystal
Compelling boats, clouds, birds.
The million whispers of fulfilment in the green ears.

Scapa Flow

Scapa Flow: great warships lie ramshackle
Under the gray floor.
And soon the veins of oil will throb and flow.

Sea and Cliffs
Sea, old sculptor, carves from the western ramparts
Stack and cave and skerry,
Sweep harpist, with sagas of salt and stone.

Fishing Bird
It waits, rock-fast, wind-flung
Wing – wind – enthirling
One flash from the sea's hoard.

Island Faces
Many masks merge here, in an island face –
Pict, Norseman, Scot
Face of a crofter, gnawed with loam
Face of fishermen, seamen –
Gray of the sea, eyes level as horizons.

Old Houses, New Houses
The old crofts ride the green hill surges,
Long arks; man and beast under one roof.
The new houses,
Will they be there at the dove's return?

Stromness
Stromness, Hamnavoe – 'haven inside the bay'
Twenty stone piers, with boats,
A street uncoiling like a sailor's rope.

Fishermen and Crofters
They hold the keys to earth and ocean,
Earth-key, the plough;
Sea-opener, the net and sinker;

Seventy years nourished with corn and fish,
They open the mysterious doors,
Go, most into earth,
A few through the door of the sea.
They gain the richness of man through the elements.

June 1976

The Bridegroom from the Sea

I stopped at 'The Arctic Whaler'
To give me courage,
Also to hire a horse, Bess, at the yard.

There was that ale-house in Kirbister.
Bess wouldn't pass the door
Till we'd dug our faces deep in the grain.

Aith in Sandwick, what horseman
Could ever resist your malt?
I sat at the fire with four thirsty ploughmen.

I'd deserted *Susie*, my yawl, that day
To bespeak a bride,
A Birsay lass, well dowered.

I was wearing my best black suit.
At Dounby, didn't I set the mothballed elbow
In a pool of sour ale?

The deeper that nag bore me
Among the barley fields
The sweeter the sea sang in my ears.

Good reports of that lass –
Bonny, a baker of good bread,
A golden hand in the butter-kirn.

After the shebeen in Marwick
I had to rest in a ditch.
I woke up. Bess was away in a green wind.

I never stood at that bride's door.
I footed it home to Hamnavoe.
I said to my boat next morning,

'*Susie*, sweetheart, forgive me.
Our creels never lacked a lobster.
Your thwarts thrashed with continuous silver.

'Brutish servitude, hooves and millstones.
You and I, *Susie*, will go still
Among the blue-and-silver coursers out west.'

1992

The Bridegroom

He spurred round the hill Kringlafiold,
Reined in his horse at croft and croft,
   Chanted the summons, was offered
   The messenger's ale-cup,

Then on, the beast flinging foam on the wind
(Wind blowing foam from ale-cup and ale-cup),
   By way of the marsh and granite,
   To the terrace of scattered crofts

Above Hoy Sound and the shining west,
Garth, Feolquoy, Don, Lingmira,
   Liffea, Legar, Dale,
   Weaverhall, Witt,

Got welcome at every door, but after
The heavy malt of Don, had wisdom
   To froth his beard only,
   And at Pow, horse clomping cobbles,

'Bring your fiddle,' added to the bell cry,
Then dropped down to Glebe, between
   Oatfield and barley
   To where Mr Clouston, minister,

Was taking combs from a hive, addressing
The firestorm of bees in Latin, with

'Sir, if you please, we want
The wedding on Lammas Tuesday.'

And set a shilling in the web of sticky fingers.
Then put the scatter of hooves about
   And up across the ridge
   To Castle, Croval, Langhouse,

And sat for oatcakes and cheese at Hammar
(The horse's tongue dredging the trough).
   The west smouldered, stars
   Were sketching a silver rune,

While the bridegroom lingered, and lamps
Stood in Hamnavoe windows,
   Blond squares, and a homing boat
   Struggled in the tide's honey.

3 August 1988

The Tryst

'Kirsten' . . . (A moth-burr at a window.)
Kirsten stirs in a caul of shadows.

'Kirsten, I'm outside, it's cold.'
Kirsten sleeps, on her cheek the warm moon apple.

'Kirsten, it's me, Sander.'
Kirsten is in a country that knows no names.

'Kirsten, I've ridden four miles through the gale.'
Through Kirsten's skull it falls, a silver rain.

'Kirsten, I've brought you this rose.'
Kirsten trundles a little bee in her nostril.

'Kirsten, you promised! – O Kirsten – Kirsten!'
In a crystal cave lies Kirsten, sweetly cloistered.

February 1979

Elizabeth Sweyn, widow, at her writing desk in the hall

For taking a trout out of my water: the cold hill
   water that tumbles white and brown over stones
   to the loch, and loses itself there awhile, and
   then gathers its strands and issues out again,
   tranquil and blue and reed-stained, to the sea,
      I summon you to the Hall.

For making much noise in the bothies and beyond about
   the French and their setting to rights of the
   frame of society (wrenched from its natural
   frame by priest and tyrant): and so casting
   a shadow of doubt and threat and disquiet upon
   this ancient island seat, and sowing mischiefs
   in simple minds,
      I summon you to the Hall.

For arrears of rent. I have had much patience with
   that old perverse one, your mother, who has
   not two farthings to tinkle together when it
   comes to Martinmas and the factor stands in
   the office with his open rent-book and the
   crofters come in, one by one, silver-fingered,
   taking off their bonnets: no, but the same
   bold lady could come back from last Lammastide
   in Kirkwall with a new bonnet and gloves, and
   a dozen white cups and plates with blue scroll-
   work on them: and after cries to Mr Brodie my
   grieve, *What way at all can I pay, and that*
   Stephen of mine never turning tilth, no but

squandering every sea-sillock-cent in the ale-
house, morning to night, year-long?
    I summon you to the Hall.

You understand well enough, it's bred in your bone,
    it is as sure rooted in every person in this island
    as the order and priority of stars – one fish
    in seven, and that the best, is to be left at
    the door of the Hall before sunset: and you
    have gone by the door of the Hall every night
    this past moon with a string of cod in your
    finger to some ignorant red-mouth and sweet-
    whisperer in a darkling hill croft; and so
    left my five cats hungry.
    I summon you to the Hall.

For continual disrespect, in that when a certain
    person is horse-borne on the island road all
    islanders but one doff bonnets, and crook the
    knee, and cast their eyes down; no, but one
    certain lump of obstinate clay turns his back,
    yea and falls to studying a bird's flight, or
    a flower opening, or a raindrop in a pool:
    for explanation of such and other practisings
    and slightings
    I summon you to the Hall.

For that all summonses hitherto, delivered by sundry:
    as, the factor Mr Walter, the grieve John-
    William Brodie, Hilda the lass from the
    butter-house here, Ikey the tinker who passes
    word about the crofts in consideration of a
    sup of whisky, Mr Gilfillan the new minister,

the Hall dog Major (who so delicately carries
letters in his teeth), since all and every
summons from here has been a summons to a
stone, I intend to come with this myself,
unfaltering from Hall to hovel, six black
words on a white sheet,
    I summon you to the Hall
For a hundred reasons I cannot think of now, man,
    I summon you to the Hall.

You have hair like spillings of sunlight and the
    distant words of your mouth laughing among
    fishermen are a disturbance to me and (I know
    it) when you walk from your mother's door of
    mornings to the boat *Cloud-racer* the island
    seems to be yours then, and not this foolish
    widowed soon-to-wither woman's; and if I do
    not speak soon, some little slut from the hill
    or the shore will have you to kirk and to bed
    and to bairn-making; and what is authority in
    a place if a yoke cannot be put on a serf, a
    mere mingling of brief dust and spume; no
    hard yoke either, but a sweet yoke of ease and
    privilege; that being undeniably so?
    I . . .

        *

Mrs Sweyn, the young widow, left off her writing
here, she smiled, she tore her letter into small
pieces and let them fall and flutter from her
hand into the coal-fire in the study.

1978–80

Unlucky Boat

That boat has killed three people. Building her
Sib drove a nail through his thumb. He died in his croft
Bunged to the eyes with rust and penicillin.
One evening when the Flow was a bar of silver
Under the moon, and Mansie and Tom with wands
Were putting a spell on cuithes, she dipped a bow
And ushered Mansie, his pipe still in his teeth,
To meet the cold green angels. They hauled her up
Among the rocks, right in the path of Angus,
Whose neck, rigid with pints from the Dounby Market,
Snapped like a barley stalk . . . There she lies,
A leprous unlucky bitch, in the quarry of Moan.

Tinkers, going past, make the sign of the cross.

1971

49

A New House

They shall sit at the fire,
Neighbour and tramp
And such as seek shelter from the sea.

A fiddle at the wall.
A deep bed.
In the cupboard, a loaf and a bottle.
The Word in the window.
Two cows, ladies of butter, in the long silk summer grasses.

Twelve sheep on the hill.
At the lee wall
Net and plough and peatstack.

And a lucky boat on the shore.

May the rat in the field be chaste and a lover of thistles.

1967

The Guardians

May a strong guardian
Stand at the door
With sword and olive branch.

May the keeper of the windows
Be eager-eyed
For dawn and the first star,
   snow-light and corn-light.

May the keeper of the fire
See a loaf on the table
And faces of travellers lit with welcome
   and shadow-of-flame, in winter.

May the keeper of the beds be resolute
Against the terror that walks by night,
And herd with gentleness the flocks of sleep.

In a blue-and-silver morning
On the first winter step
Those guardians, and others who hold a finger
     to the lip, smiling
Came about her who holds now the key of the house.

1989

The Finished House

In the finished house a flame is brought to the hearth.
Then a table, between door and window
Where a stranger will eat before the men of the house.
A bed is laid in a secret corner
For the three agonies – love, birth, death –
That are made beautiful with ceremony.
The neighbours come with gifts –
A set of cups, a calendar, some chairs.
A fiddle is hung at the wall.
A girl puts lucky salt in a dish.
The cupboard will have its loaf and bottle, come winter.
On the seventh morning
One spills water of blessing over the threshold.

1968

Cragsmen

Cragsman
He wears the long blue wind for a coat.

Shyness
Wart is such a shy boy
He turns aside
From hag or honeymouth or even a small girl on the
    road.
Wart has taken, though,
The she-kestrel in his fist.

Pinleg
Sam'l fell, broke his leg.
He sat a morning
Among broken gull-eggs, shattering waves.
Now (lacking his leg)
He breaks burning peats with a long wooden toe.

Hatchling
Tammag said to the naked thing
Blinking
Out of a broken shell,
'You and me, buddo,
May have business with each other
In a twelvemonth maybe.'

Cliff Fall

No. Never look. Is no
Kist or kirkyard stone for Mansie.
Seventeen summers corn-lissom
He plummeted
To meet the singing seagirls.
One bore him off, brided him
In a cell beyond Hoy or Suleskerry.

Fight

'This was my bird
And my eggs. I was eyeing
This ledge since last winter . . .'
'No, but the bird
Stretched her neck into my hand,
The bird
Kissed my neck – look – till it bled . . .'
That cliff talk
Came to flung fists, torn blood, later
In the horizontal ale-house
As if a stinking fulmar
Had been Jean of Fea, bonniest of the lasses that year.

The Test

Before a cragsman can put a ring on a girl's finger
Let him
Teeter on one leg on a high ledge,
Launch himself
Up and round in a wheel
And stand (fluttering)
Facing the bird-hung crag-face,
The mother, gaunt
Giver of life and death.

The Last Step
And Bertak said,
'I know every step in that crag.'
And he said,
'I could go up and down
Blindfold.'
And avouched, into his third mug of ale,
'I don't need a star either.'
He said,
'I think I work better without women.'
That same winter
Bertak went up with a full sack of eggs.
There was a bud of love in his heart.
On the last step
Rose and eggs and Bertak went their ways.

The Challenge
Once I had a race with Andro
Up the crag.
Andro, being first, got
Marget for wife, the lass
That was half a swan.
I kiss, forty winters on,
The wrinkled cheek and chin of the Gray Head.

Dunce
Ten mistakes in grammar! Two
Multiplications wrong!
'Helsingfors,' I stammered, 'capital of Greece . . .'
I was thrust
Forth from the House of Learning, a dunce.

I hung, all morning,
Between a wave and a cloud.

Home-sickness
Chaldru is back from New York.
Mother and father and sisters
And brother
He left behind in America
(The brother
With a desk job in a lawyer's office in Boston).
'I missed the cliffs,' said Chaldru,
Lighting a fire in the ruin of the old croft.

The Bigger Cliffs
'I have to say,' said James the fisherman
In the reeking ale-house,
'Hoy has higher crags than ours.'
And Chaldru's ship
Had passed St Kilda, going to New York.
'Cloud-rakers, star-rakers . . .'
That night
James and Chaldru bought their own booze.

A Drowning
He struggled into a gray and silver coat of sea.

For Jean of Fea: A Love Song
An egg or two for the minister.
Three eggs for the factor.
And a hatful
For Sam'l to crack on his wooden leg.
An egg for Blind Magso

And one for Skatehorn the tramp.
Where
(Among what reeds, on what lost islet)
Will I get me a swan's egg to take to a croft
On the far side of Fea?

Crag Talk
   'Seapink, bonny lass, is this thee . . .?'
   'Mistress Fulmar, spitting stink at me,
   Tonight
   Jean will break two of your eggs in the spitting pan . . .'
   'Mister Limpet,
   What news in your tent today?'
   The crag
   Whispered and laughed and thundered
   Red answers all about Kelpie.

Relics
   'If I die,' said Kelpie,
   (For maybe death's a dream
   Everybody dreams
   Except the withering man himself)
   'Put me under the hill
   With a few raven-shells and the skull of a gannet.'

Last Cragsman
   Nobody knows
   The way down the red stair now
   But myself and Kelpie
   (I wouldn't put it past that new taxman)
   And the nose-twitcher (the rabbit)
   And the tinker's old goat.

House of Sea Stones
  Sig drove his wife and two daughters the long way
      round
  To the foot of the Gray Head
  And up again, salt stones in their baskets,
  To build his croft.
  (That was a hundred years ago.
  In a sea-haar, the floor-stones shine like mirrors.)

Schoolmaster
  'The prudent ones, they plough and they
  Gather into barns . . .'
  'The average ones, they
  Hammer planks together with nails, they fish . . .'
  'A few, the best,
  Sit at an office desk in Kirkwall with soap-bright
      fingers . . .'
  'About the gatherers of crag-fruit
  I have nothing to say.'

Sunset
  When sun meets sea
  The crag is twelve ladders of fire.
                                    Spring 1983–August 1995

Peter Maxwell Davies: 60
8 September 1994

There: the Rackwick boats
Are round Rora now
(See the patched sails, how
    They drink the wind!)

And the women count sixty
    boxes on the
    stones: haddock,
    cod, a huge
    halibut.

Summer's end: the patched
Fields of Rackwick
        Hold sixty stooks, in
    burnished ranks.
    No one in the valley
Will lack bread and porridge
    At the time of the first snow.

Orpheus in his cottage
    Near the crag edge
Ponders
The mystery of being and time; all
    His years a net
Of dancing numbers and notes.
    But sixty: this September
    All the birds of Hoy will sing blithely.

15 August 1994

59

Achievement

The Old Man of Hoy (455 feet) was first climbed in 1966. These lines celebrate a much later American ascent of the famous sea stack.

Through spindrift, blizzarding birds,
The salt-eaten stone,
And the great bell of the Atlantic
Beating far below,

They have broken now
Into the high wind and the sun,
Where the eagle
Might linger in the great arc of
            his flight, to salute them.

1987

The Rackwick Dove

A pigeon was hurled from its course
Into the valley of salt and corn . . .

Will it leap over the hill's shoulder again?
Ah, it hasn't the strength.

Bide awhile then, bird of peace,
About the thresholds of Rackwick.

The bird hesitates between sixteen gables.
Too many crofts are empty skulls.

Go, there's Lucy up at Glen.
Lucy will scatter you crumbs galore.

The knight of music, up at Bunertoon. Sir Peter,
All birds are his friends. Fly there.

Twenty children of summer on the beach.
One could make a salt branch of her arm.

On Mucklehoose roof it flutters, falls.
Hutch has hammered a fish-box house.

Alan threw grain on the flagstones.
It lived like a prince on gold tithes.

But it pined for the broken flight,
Longed for the lost gray company.

After breakfast, one morning, we find
It has shaken our abundant salt from its wings.

13 July 1987

Gossip in Hamnavoe: About a Girl

'I tell you, man,
A mermaid's been taken in the nets!
Go along to the fishermen's pier.'

'She must be somebody from the fair –
The girl
They draw a star of flaming daggers round.'

'Oh no, no. I think she's
The new minister's niece, a bonny lass,
On holiday from the college.'

'A girl with honey-coloured hair?
No girl like that here.
Oh, who's the princess at the end of the close?'

'The pity is, a girl's beauty
Stacks in this heart and that
Such honey-loads of pain.'

'One old poet doesn't grumble. She
Quickened a dead tree.
His pen flowered among the gales and snow.'

'Oh, she'll be back. That dear one
Is gold of our corn,
She's Orkney rain and spindrift . . .'

31 January 1987

A Hamnavoe Man

A child in a sea-close, the salt on his tongue

A boy on a pier, taut dripping line
and twist of silver (a sillock)

A young man under Yesnaby, saving
creels from the purpling west

A man and a woman, lamplight, the
plate with haddock and tatties
and butter, and the bairn in
the boat-shaped cradle

An old man on a fish-box
smoking his pipe,
eyes level as horizon

The stone in the kirkyard
The voices of ocean all around.

October 1991

The Old Woman in Number 20

Sons? I'll tell you about my five sons.
The oldest, Bill,
He keeps a sweetie shop at the end of the street.
He visits with a half-pound of tea at the weekend
And a packet of Rich Tea biscuits.
His wife hoards every ha'penny.
She stopped visiting a year ago,
We'd had words.

Dick, he's a fisherman. Well,
I never lack for haddocks.
Martha, his wife, she comes with fish in a pot, up the pier,
And tatties laced golden with butter.
And they have eight growing bairns.

Andrew, he's the clever one.
Andrew stands at a blackboard in the school at Norday,
Smelling of chalk and ink.
His Edinburgh wife, she's too grand to visit.

One morning thirty winters ago
Sam's bed was empty. I got
One letter from Napier, New Zealand. Silence ever since.
Bert Wylie the sailor saw Sam once
On the wharfs of Dunedin, patches on his coat.

Poor Jimmag, he's no good to anybody, except
He might take me a bunch of mayflowers from a ditch.

He's never had a job.
I give him a pound from my pension
Every weekend for a pint and a packet of Woodbines.

February 1992

Kirk Bell

Dove, unfurled 'twixt ark and sun,
Give Sabbath tongue!

Folk wind-burdened, folk wind-blown.
Dang-dang, ding-dong.
Birds howk long worms from the lawn.
The bronze vibrates.

A family goes, one long black line.
It romps and reels, the steeple.

Old Tabby licks the kipper bone.
'Come pray, good people!'

Six fine hats down one small lane,
The high mouth brims, berates.

The organ preludes, a solemn paean.
The bell is a folded dove again.

1985

Fundamentalist

An ordinary day in the parish

The pub opened and shut
A hen quizzed a dandelion
One swan lit the water

Everything was in its place

But Amos crossed the hill
Certain that arks, pillars of salt, apocalyptic beasts
Would any moment
Cover the boring landscape.

1961

Old Tins

Be reverent, dustman.
   That tin
Was Spain and oranges,
   And that
The Atlantic samurai, the lobster.
   And there
With an ignorant yell you throw,
Among ashes and *Sunday Posts*,
The holy cell where brooded

   The bruised monk Barleycorn

   Who shrived our thirsts.

March 1961

Neighbours

When I've uttered the old grave words in the true order,
Maurya
Goes gravely across the field between our two doors.
I know the things mouthed
In that cottage with the wireless aerial.
The crofter is saying, 'I told you,
Keep away from that old liar, the cat wife.'
And the mother,
'Bedtime and not a schoolbook opened!'
The black Ford, like a shark,
Has taken the brother into its maw of oil and rust.
Old Grand-da tells (but nobody listens)
How a boy and a girl – neighbours – raked pools
In the golden time, for whelks and mussels . . .
Maurya sets a first daffodil
In a jam jar in her window.
Hesper hangs a lantern over the sea.

What it is to be an old one going with her rune
On the long road between flower and star.

11 May 1988

The Mother

On Monday she stood at the wooden wash-tub,
Suds to the elbow,
A slave among the storm-gray shirts and sheets.

Tuesday, she pegged the washing high –
The garden a galleon in a gale!
Then lamplight, the iron, the crisp sun-smelling folds.

The rooms thrummed with Gaelic rhythms,
A low monotone, on a Wednesday
(And every day), ancient Celtic work-spells.

She was never free like the lipsticked shop-girls
On Thursday afternoon; all her tasks
Were like bluebells in a jar on the window-sill.

On Friday she rose above textures of oat and barley
Into the paradise of cakes.
I licked cream from the wooden spoon.

Saturday night, I followed her basket and purse.
The grocer, silver-spectacled, was king
Of the apples, cheeses, syrup, sweetie-jars, cloves.

We sat, seven, in the high pew on Sunday.
After the psalms, her paper poke
Made sweet thunders all through the sermon.

1995

Many church-going families depended on a poke of sweets to survive the longueurs *of the traditional Presbyterian sermon. In his autobiography,* For the Islands I Sing, *the author remarks that 'the rustling of the bag sounded like a small electric storm in the pauses of the minister's discourse'.*

Trees

A certain child is out of the island,
Her with spillings-of-sunlight hair.
She has gone to the city.
The old man, thin from stokeholds,
Ventures as far as the peatstack.
Every house but one
Has had its postcard, blots and chunks of script.
Dogs bark lonely. Wind blows poorer, I swear.
You would see his black beard on the shore
In a smoulder of sunset, faced south.
(The ring of pure elements that is an island
Suffers a breach
From the subtraction of sweet bright dust.)
The road goes idle from north to east.
Occasionally
It has some unimportant person on it.

*

Emmeline is back! She has taken the skyway home.

*

Women from every croft but one
Troop to the door of new experience.
Their tongues ring with welcome in the threshold,
Nine separate bellmouths.
You can see, in the dark corner, the cheese-cutter cap.

73

(Hong Kong to Leith,
He has wandered by many forests of masts.)
He asks no questions.
He sparks fierce matches at an unbroken pipe.
The mouths of the women peal with inquisition.
'The house I lived in was high as a crag.'
'The clouds under the wing
Were just like the froth in Merran's ale-bin.'
'Three whole days
I could not know what the wife in the sweetie shop said.'
'A blind man with a quick white stick.'
'Did you like the postcards I sent?'
'There was this one gray patch of sky
Above the Castle.'
'And one day we walked through a wood.'
'Never a sheep or a cow or pig,
Just red shapes on a hook.'
'I bought that pipe for Grandad. Look.'

*

The women go, their ears brimming with marvels.
The old one endures his varnished pipe.
She's in her nightgown soon.
She lights a candle.
   Kisses the beard.
     Whispers.
'I hope I dream about the trees all night.'

He nods beside the glow of a bog-drowned forest.
He puffs on till the pipe is sweet.

1975

The Sons and Daughters of Barleycorn

THE YOUNG MEN

The Griefs of the Young Men

1

I swore, after the third pint,
  To lift more creels than Thorf –
  Crammed every Yesnaby creel with the blue lobster
    fruit.
Thorf, six boxes despatched in ice to Billingsgate,
  Was buying whisky to all the fishermen in 'The Arctic
    Whaler'.

I drank the sixth pint, alone.

When I launched the *Whitemaa*
  After the tenth pint of Flett's strongest ale,
We ended on the reef Hellyan.
Whitemaa and I
A laughing stock in Hamnavoe all that winter.
'Twenty pounds,' said Stanger the boatbuilder,
'To fit a new strake.'

Whitemaa, smashed, still lies on the noust.

I signed on with Thorf at the end of December.

I have lost my boat and my lass.

'Listen,' said Mr Stove, the factor.
'Listen well.
Listen to what I have to say, man.

We had no trouble at all with your father,
That good man who's dead.
You should think shame
Whenever you pass your father's grave in the kirkyard,
Unquiet dust.

You didn't mend the hill dyke after lambing.
Swine snortled in the burn.
The white bull
Stood throat-deep in the green oats.
The first summer wind
Blew down your scarecrow.
More seriously,
You have paid no rent for the croft Leaquoy,
Neither in May nor Michaelmas.
Do you want to stand out on the road
With your goat and six hens
And your mother's sticks of furniture . . . ?'

How can I tell the old scum, all summer
    I've been pleading with Peterina of Smelt,
And if Peterina marries me
Leaquoy will be like a ship in a green sea?

3

The registrar licked his pencil
And wrote 'Andrew James' in his register.

'How many sons is it you have now, William?' says he.

'Ten sons,' said I,
'And three lasses.'

'Well,' said the registrar,
'You look in the dumps. Have
A drop from my phial?'

He blew stoor and a spider
Out of two dirty glasses.

When I topped the hill
I could see the five youngest
Brawling about in the barnyard.

I got to the stile. The dog barked.
My wife, Jemima,
Was singing above the small bagpipes
Of Andrew James, our newborn.

4

But when I got to the wreck
The hold was a wooden cave, sloshing sea.

Every pig-sty and empty well
Stuffed with apples
And kegs of Swedish spirits.

I thought to get a few baulks of wood
To make tables, a door,
A few rafters to keep the roof solid.

77

(No timber so seasoned
As Baltic merchantmen.)

Then the factor arrived
And four excisemen from Kirkwall.

5

I was signing on for a whaler.
The quill in my fist.
Stumbling, stammering across the page,
Scattering blots,
When a shadow fell on the book.

I followed my mother like
A young dangerous dog
Back to plough, peat-bog, crab creels.

6

Blood in the beer! I sat
   All weekend in the Hamnavoe jail
For fighting with Thorf, my friend . . .

About? Lobsters or lasses or the Liberal candidate,
I forget. I must
   Stand in the dock on Tuesday first.

7

The *Albion* on Graemsay. I turned
   A swathe of seaweed
And there a face remote as a star,
The mouth strung with hair.

I think I'll grow to be an old man,
And that star
Trembling in the rockpool always.

The Joys of the Young Men

1

Last winter I drained the bog.
  It had drowned, lately,
  A dog and a ram.
  Now it's a patch of young corn.

2

A hard thing, being
  Small and ugly, and a heart
  Like red iron, with love, in a forge.

And a strong coarse brute
  Coaxing her, ignorant urgings,
  At Harvest Home outside
  Under the cold stars.

And winter fell on the red iron.
  Rose leaves spilt on my hand,
  Standing in the kirk beside her.

And the coarse brute, the ploughman,
  Trudged to the smithy
  To get him a strong plough.

3

Three years since I rented the shop
Lic^d to sell Tobacco and Spirits –
Choicest Indian Teas – Coffee
Fresh-ground on the Premises

With the few sovereigns
My poor grannie kept in a kist under the bed.

I dropped the plough in the furrow
The day she died
And walked the six miles to Hamnavoe, to the lawyer
    there.

I spent a month sweeping cobwebs from a hovel,
Nagging a joiner
To make wood shavings curl and whisper
For counter and shelves,
Licking a pen
With lists for the wholesale merchant, commercial
    travellers.

This morning
The bank agent was smiling like a sour lemon – 'Mister
    Halcro,
You've made three hundred pounds this year.'

4

I woke up. The croft
Had winged up near the sun, into pure dazzlement.

I opened the door,
The hill was a white whale.

I dug seven ewes out of seven blinding graves
Before the old wife
Cried, *The broth's on the table.*

Her withered face, that snowfall,
Shone like an angel.

The three bairns building the snowman,
Their mouths shivered like small silver bells.

5

I am the laird's son
And I am new out of Lancing.
I ride my chestnut over the parish
And the crofters' women
Bow shawled heads on Greenay Hill,
When Sven, my horse, strikes a spark from a stone,
   Going with my gun after grouse.

Today a girl in an oatfield
   Made no curtsy,
     She looked me flush in the teeth, unsmiling.

I smiled, going on the sheep-path with my falcon.

I think I won't tell my father
He has a radical virago on his estate.
   'Worse than the black worm,' he'd say.

How shall I find out the name of the temptress?

81

6

'Drunk and incapable. Assault and battery.
Resisting arrest.
Together with co-accused Thorfinn Voe, fisherman.'

The sheriff had a beetroot face, only
Brandy and port wine
Could have patched his cheeks that colour.

The sheriff listened merrily to Swann the publican
                              and Dass the constable
And witnesses, a few fawners and lick-boots.

The sheriff shuffled papers.

The sheriff looked at Thorf and me, Thorf
Says 'sternly', but
As sure as I sit here, in 'The Crab and Creel'
With my dram and scooner of ale,
That sheriff winked at us.

'*Not proven*,' says the sheriff.

And down he brought his gavel on the bench
Such a smack
I thought it might take two joiners
A fortnight to patch the woodwork.

7

The old women at the pier steps,
Cleaning fish

In a demented blizzard of wings
– 'That gull furling his wings,
   That's Peter Thomson . . .'
'It might be or it mightn't
   But I ken Bert Isbister
Though he's a whitemaa
And lacks a clay pipe in his beak . . .'
– 'I know Willag Simpson.
He made
That exact same outcry
Every Saturday night, being
Thrown out of 'The White Horse'.
Here, Willag, whitemaa, here's
A tail and a fin for thee . . .'
So my mother and the pier women,
Putting a name to every gull,
A fisherman dead or drowned.

And here I am
Setting my basket of cod on the pier steps,
Alive and in love,
Just before the old women come in a flock with flashing
      tongues and knives.

The Young Men at the Hamnavoe Lammas Market

1

'Fish,' said the old wife, 'I swear
   I can hear choirs of them in the mouth of Hoy Sound
      Pleading for the hooks!'

But I put on my black suit
   And I took five shillings and threepence –
      ha'penny from the loose stone in the wall
And I set out for the Fair.

My mother, Jane 'Clip-cloots', raged at the end of the
     close.

2

'No,' said I to Bella-Ann,
'I'll darken the door of not one ale-house.
   You must bide and milk the cow.
   You must be here
When the bairns come home from the school.'

'Last Lammas,' says Bella-Ann,
   'You darkened seven pub doors in Hamnavoe
   And when the sun was still high
The pubs had put complete darkness on you, man.'

I all but went on my knees to Bella-Ann.

In the end we trailed into Hamnavoe, me
   And Bella-Ann and the five bairns.
   We passed the doors of pub after pub.
Even when Bella-Ann slipped away
   To have her fortune told
   (Secret words, shadow of silver on a hand)
I couldn't get near the doors
Brimming like hives
For the five laughing howling coconut-gnawing kids.

The steamer *Hoy Head* from Hoy, Flotta, Fara, Graemsay
  Full of folk,
  The men in black suits, every lass
Like a butterfly from the laird's garden,
Their mouths all rose curls and dew.

The coaches from Birsay, Harray, Sandwick, Stenness,
Likewise laden.

And I at the coal store
Shovelling a mountain of coal into hundredweight sacks,
  Black as the King of Africa,
  Black as the marketman licking the red-hot poker.

4

The most wonderful thing I ever saw
  – And I stuck a harpoon in four whales last summer
  In Davis Straits,
Besides lifting a thousand creels in the west,
  Purple with lobsters,
  Like ancient knights in dungeons,
And passing a million haddock and herring
Through slime-silvered hands –
  Most amazing,
A little fish yellow as a Chinaman
  Gowping and gaping
  Round and round in a small glass bowl.

All the world's in Hamnavoe this day –
A line of Indians selling silks,
Charlie Rigolo, Italian, whirling his wheel and numbers,

Six Jews with their shooting booths (china teapots for
    prizes),
The Prince of the Congo
In a leopard coat crying 'alabakalavia',
The Persian fortune-teller
With planets and a black cat painted on her booth,
Guilio with the ice-cream barrow,
Cockneys and gypsies and Mrs Gold from Germany.

Jock the sailor says
    You wouldn't see the like of this throng
    On any waterfront, 'Frisco to Shanghai.

6

I thought this, spurring Betsy
    Through the Scorradale gap
    To the masks and the music,
'Now the root has drunk the rain
    First green shoot
    Is soaked in sunlight,
        The tall bronze whisperer
Is a dancer in the wind,
    And all stand stooked
Against the white siege of winter.
    It was Betsy's hoof
That spanned the ripening summer
    (Betsy is my mare)
Hlafmas – Lammas – 'feast of the loaf'.

Feet that have ploughed, feet
    That have followed the scythe,
Come in in hundreds to dance on this day,

Throats sun-dry, devout,
To tap the barley oozings.

7

The nine parishes are here
   And the five islands,
A thousand faces
   Patched red with drink and laughter.
   And I go all day
Seeking one face like a star.
   There it was, red under a flare
Taking a coarse kiss
From Jock of Curquoy, that
   Red hunk of peat-bog.

21–27 May 1991

ISLAND GIRLS

The Grief of Island Girls

1

Why am I sad,
   of all the island girls?

I have brought my pail home,
   empty from the hill.
   Buttercup the cow
   was sold last week at the mart.

2

No one saw me
   lifting my apron to my eyes

87

the day Thorf
was rowed out to the tall ship.

Darkness and dew.
Secretly, in silence, the dew falls.

3

I am not to be married
to Rob and his hundred acres
till the time of snow and stars.

I wanted
to walk across the burn to the kirk
through marigolds
and larks singing over Ernefea.

4

This the grandmother left me,
her spinning wheel,
and I expecting a bag of crowns and sovereigns
to buy a sweetie shop in Hamnavoe.

5

His fiddle woke me,
among the drunks in the village inn
– their slurpings and howlings!
I danced alone in my attic.

6

At first dawn of May
I climbed Kringlafiold,
I soaked my face in the dew.

'Merran,' says the rockpool at sunset,
   'You're as plain as ever you were.'

7

Six silly girls
   sit in the new school
   learning letters and numbers.

Soon they'll be prim
   as the lady and her daughter up at the Hall.

Because I'm fifteen
   I mend creels at the sea-wall, and spit.

Island Girls at Harvest Time

1

Oats in my hair,
   dust of oats in my mouth,
      fingers torn with sharp stalks.

I'm half blinded too
   with the flaming scythe in front.

I would sit down, but Tomas
   goes on and on,
   circled with flame from knee to shoulder.

2

Why do I have to bide here
   stirring bitters in a black pot?

89

All the island lasses
  are out in the sun and wind
  bending, binding sheaves.

'Merran, your turn this year
  to brew ale for the Harvest Home.'

3

Jessie goes round with the last oatcakes.
  There's a black cloud over the sun
  like the patch on a sailor's eye.

Betsy drives the cork
  into the stone ale-jar.

The men sharpen the blades on a stone.
  The blades are dull.
  Jean holds out a hand for the first raindrop.

4

Benna, foolish creature,
  has scattered a sheaf,
gone screaming
  from a rat unlocked from its green house
  by a singing scythe.

5

Betsy is princess today.
  All the valley crofters
  are cutting her father's barley.

Betsy stands in the door of Garth
   with the ale-crock
   and the basket of cheese and oatcakes.
Betsy, princess,
   will bestow gifts on the sweating serfs.

The old queen
mutters inside. She counts pennies and shillings.

                    6
'How many bannocks in this field?'
A thousand.
'And how many tubs of ale?'
A hundred or more.

And somewhere, hidden, the oats
that will make the oatcake
that will be broken
above the head of a winter bride.

                    7
There was only one shower, at noon.
The uncut oats
were hung with raindrops.

   Now the field's all cut.

'Tomas, come up to the ale-house.'

   Tomas lingers beside a corngold girl,
   She sucks a drop of blood from her finger.

The Joy of Island Girls

1

Look, Madda! – a puff of smoke!
  – the *Hoy Head*
  from Hamnavoe coming
  with chocolates, apples, bottles of scent,
    and ribbons from the Lammas fair.

2

I unlocked the door this morning.
  A great trout lay streaming on the step.

3

If you go by the croft of Quoy
  Tell Andrina
there'll be two places at this table.
Tell that girl
the old mother who baked the cake won't be there.

4

I unlatched my door one morning
  and covered my eyes!
My bridelace so dingy in the dazzle of new snow.

5

Dawn and a stiff westerly.
  Three fishermen, my brothers, on the rock, teetering.
  I scattered them with a word.
    I came back with twenty lobsters.

Rob and Jock and Mansie
   were in the ale-house.

And I hauled up *Fulmar*, alone.

6

I unlatched the door.
Tessa the tinker read in my hand
a town house, horses and a coach,
a golden beard,
a desk and ledgers in Hamnavoe.

Well, it only cost sixpence.
Tessa's palm wasn't rich like mine.

7

They stopping the peat-heave at noon,
   the women went here and there
with oatcakes and ale.
Sando said, *That pot with the blue stripe going round it,*
   it has the best ale.

The faces of the women
   would have soured a honeycomb.
   Three went home, unbidden.

When Sando lifted his face from the wet black bank
   I wanted to give it a sunset kiss.

27 September 1987/1993/1995

Shrove Tuesday

The fiddlers, they were suddenly there,
Three fiddlers
More eager for ale than dances.
'The cloth's not off the kirn yet . . .'
'The sun's still up . . .'
They stamping feet with rage!
Then Merran brought to the barn a lantern.
The old fiddler
Stoked his thirst at the farm fire.
His two boys went out to the hill to gather in girls.
(The ox stood, a black flame, in the winter byre.)

Soon were fifty under the barn rafters,
Under the russet splash of the lantern.
Six farm women
Going with baked fish and bannocks on a board,
Merran following with the ale-bowl,
The old dragging in from the twilight like snails
The children a wheel and whirl of birds.
And all laughing,
The young fiddler lost, last seen
Black against sunset bars.
(The farmer stood alone,
Solemn between harness and harrows.)

Too much should not be said about that night.
Was there merriment?
Was one bad fight, with red wet stars on the whitewash,

An old man thought him a boy again
In a whirling, skirling giggle of girls,
A child weeping in a corner,
Reel after reel on the threshing-floor,
Two fiddles throbbing,
Merran mad – the goosegirl has dropped
An ale-crock on a flagstone,
A wild flung star of malt.
'Tinkers hungry this March night, tented poorly . . .'

*

Out with them, out and off, before midnight,
Merran-herded,
Off home under The Plough,
Drunks, fiddlers, bairns on sleep fallen,
The gray-faced eld
Hirpling to a dozen doors before the last door.
(The stars like scatterings of corn seed.)
All's swept into one corner,
Crusts, fishbones, the fiddler's bonnet,
The tooth of a fighter,
The dust of twenty farms about.
Mice cheepered in the wall.
Then board and bowls to the house brought in.
The lantern lost in circles of dawn-light.
Wind of Hesper
Swept the barn of last echoes of folly.

*

Merran, hearth-bent,
Sees, beyond cold cinders, sun and bread.

Shrove Tuesday 1987

95

Ash Wednesday

Remember, man, that thou art dust.

The earl kneels, the ash of the end is written on his brow.

A captain of ships kneels, to be put in mind of a death in a
     far port, or at home, or on a rock of the sea.

And the boy that holds cinders for the priest,
His forehead is smeared,
Who wears a coat of fourteen Aprils.

The lady of Paplay
Thinks, most mornings, she will live forever; kneeling now
Is touched with the grave-stoor.

The ploughman folds sun-grained hands,
He tilts his face
To the dust drained of warmth and light.

Fisherman, the spindrift
Will wash the ashes from you tomorrow.
Still you remember, between two waves,
St Peter and the fire of his denials.

And the old bishop, 'I know this,
One God-ground deed or thought
Endures, when the circle of diamond-and-gold on my
     finger is dust.'

In the kirk of Magnus
Stood a multitude of islanders, death-farers, that day,
Hungry, after, for *panis angelicus.*

And unto dust thou shalt return.

1994

Chinoiseries

SMALL SONGS FOR THE BEGINNING OF LENT

1

Snow on Orphir hills, a shawl.
   I have broken old cake, old shortbread, on the balcony.
      And the birds dance past my window.

   The sun
   Two steps up from cinders.

Soup and bread and ale, at Hopedale,
      At two o'clock.

2

An old man has died in the House of the Old People.
They will bury him this afternoon.

He travelled far, young.
He came home to be a fisherman. At last
He was coal merchant, magistrate.

His wife died weeks ago.
   A cold burial at the end of winter.

3

The way it is with old poets: swift ebbings, swift floods.
It was a low ebb this morning,
   The spirit a beachcomber
      – Dark swathes of seaweed.

Now, after bread and honey and tea,
   Spirit urges,
      'Write a few small Lent songs.'

4

Good, the surge of the year
   Towards equinox.

Some say, winter ends with January.
   But I think it is February.
   February begins to unlatch the gate,
      Feeling with frail hands.

Still, she is the daughter of Winter,
   Cordelia of the Crocuses.

5

Two days in the valley of the shadow
   Since Ash Wednesday, two days

And still I haven't unrolled
   The chart of threnodies
     That shows a way through the place of bones
   To the garden.

Now, on the third day,
   Old bones finger the pen.

6

A hundred Lents from now
   Who will remember us?

What is a carved name, some numbers?

Sand sifts through the skulls.

Who shall know the skull of a singer?
Silence is best. Song
Should be rounded with silence.

Another tongue of dust will rejoice
A hundred springs from now.

7

Now the old sky woman
Plucks her chickens. Flakes
Drift past my window from north-west.

Between cold sunbursts
Old Bessie sits on her doorstep
And strews white feathers on the wind.

Three days into Lent,
Sun and snow mesh airily
From the hovel on Brinkie's Brae.

26 February 1993

*Bessie Millie sold favourable winds to visiting sea captains from
her hovel on Brinkie's Brae in eighteenth-century Stromness.*

Via Dolorosa: A Beggar

1

I know when there's a trial,
A sentence given.
There are three strokes on a black drum then.

2

There's always a cluster of bronze greaves,
A ring of hooves.
Today, at the roadside,
A column of pure silence.

3

Being blind, I know better than most
A butterfly lighting on a rose.
I know
When a man has stumbled on stones.

4

A rare thing in women, such silence.
(All women know it, the hour after a birth.)
Pray for me, mother, on the way.

5

Pray for the stranger
They have dragged out of the mob
To lend a hand (I know his country smells).

6

The girl from the linen shop, surely!
The unfolding,
A bright sweetness in the wind,
The fabric fallen on blood and sweat.

7

The road is steep now. The dancer
Measures his length again in the hot dust.

8

That pure silence still
Among lamentation the wildest keening I've ever known.
A penny, sir. Thank you. I think
It may come to thunder later indeed.

9

I know. I've heard it. This man
Went from hill to hill, lord of the dance.
His dance is broken today.

10

They've taken his dancing coat away.
For the patchwork coat of wounds.

11

Now they are nailing his dancing feet,
A threefold iron clang.

12

But the song goes on for three hours,
World's woe,
The psalm of the black sorrow of the shepherd king.

13

Lady, out of your death-bearing stillness,
Pray for us sinners,
All our deaths scattered through history.

14

I heard the man they are burying
Put light into a blind man's skull lately.
I am content not to see
The man evils done under the sun.
(Thank you, sir. It has been a rough day, indeed.)

16 March 1995

The Poet's Year

He can make his mouth chime –
Drops from a gray nail of ice

His silences
Are like the first cold root stirrings

His verse a trumpet in March
To widen the sun circles

Children come in a dance to his images:
Daffodil, lamb, lark

He wears the lyric coat
Cut from blue bales of sea and sky

He has knowledge of furrows
Beyond ploughmen

Can thrift sing, can herring?
He tongues their pink and silver silences

Sweeter than beeplunder, oozing,
The fairground fiddle

He knows the horncall, near sunset
For Hesper and Orion

He goes by stubble fields,
Tongue rich with shadows

He graves names of the dead
Deeper than kirkyard stones

What now, midwinter bellmouth?
Christus natus est.

October 1986

Four Kinds of Poet

'Here, now. A new time, a new place. Write something. This is expected by publisher, readers. Try to render both actuality and soul of the place, look, and write. Quick. Time passes. The place is changing as I look and write. I wither. The place ingathers in a mesh of words. Words, keep me, keep all, now: a poem.

2

'This place is boring, like most places. There's nothing I feel inclined to say about it. When (out of boredom) I try to find equivalent words, the place changes: a fog shifts, lifts. There are the stones, piers, windows, chimneys, children of light and water that once he saw in a good dream – long forgotten: a poem.

3

'What happened here? Congregate, ghosts, among the weathered and cracked stones. Take my mouth, speak. Dance. There was nothing but ritual on earth once. I imagine ceremonies. I will make masks: among those shadows buying and selling: a poem.

4

'Creation of a word, this place. What word? The word is streaming across time, holding this place and all planets and all grains of dust in a pattern, a strict equation. I am always trying to imitate the sound and shape and power of the unknowable word. Dry whisperings: a poem.'

April 1981

December Day, Hoy Sound

The unfurled gull on the tide, and over the skerry
Unfurling waves, and slow unfurling wreckage
– The Sound today a burning sapphire bough
Fretted with mimic spring.

                              The creatures of earth
Have seasons and stations, under the quartered sun
Ploughshare and cornstalk, millwheel and grinning rags.
The December seed kneels at his frosty vigil,
Sword by his side for the long crusade to the light
In trumpeting March, with the legion of lamb and leaf.

The sea grinds his salt behind a riot of masks.

Today on Hoy Sound random blossoms unfurl
Of feather and rust, a harlequin spring.

                              Tomorrow
The wave will weep like a widow on the rock,
Or howl like Lear, or laugh like a green child.

1959

A Song for Winter

'Go,' said the bird to the boy.
'Go 'down to the ship now.'

  Far the shore, bitter the salt,
  Beautiful the long curve of ocean, and
    the islands a broken string of emeralds.
  The bird fluttered about the mast
  Or sat, furled,
    Or sang at night to him on watch.

He was set ashore
  With a flute and a purse of silver.
That island
  Was a great mountain in the sea.
  'Give your strength to the mountain . . .'

He gave his songs
  To the striking of a road through high snows,
  To star configurations,
  To talk with eagles and goatherds,
Then saw below him
  Village roofs that shone in the green sun.
  The bird
Sang of girls and apples and flagons.

How long at the inn? He sat long
  Among the guitars,
  Among card games and tobacco pipes.

Autumn flames showed the branching blue of his veins.
   The talk of the men
Edged with danger and enchantment.
His silver sea-wealth
Melted like snow, and no bird sang.
   And his flute was broken.

A daughter of music
Took the withered hand of the voyager
   To a narrow house
With a tree and a well
   And a lamp on the table.
   'Here is the place, father.
   Here you must write the story.'

He laboured over the page, a hundred cold words.
   (His flute was lost.)
   He slept. When he woke
   The lamp and the fire were out.
It was the dazzling solstice of winter.
On the tree outside
   The lost bird sang.
'We have come to the place, friend.
   Tomorrow, bell and candle,
   A light, a silence
Further than sun-keel and star-chart.'

1994

The Warbeth Brothers at Christmas

The remains of a monastic chapel can still be seen in the old Stromness Kirkyard at Warbeth. It features in many of the author's poems, and most prominently in his novel Vinland.

1

We have wandered, unfaithful
Even at ploughtime
Leaving the ox in the half-made furrow.

And in the time of green shoots
We turned away
From the black wings, from worm in the root.

We presumed
To sit and eat with harvesters at lowsing-time.

Now, in the time of blackness and hunger,
Do not forget us.
Lantern and hay are brought to the ox.

2

Wake us, midnight bell, from our dreaming.
Turn us
From the comfort of the five folded senses.

Let the first unbroken snow
Take the prints of our foot.

We would go out soon
Bearing a sheaf of unlit candles under a cold star.

3

Did we not always return to the seed sack?
We did not suffer the plough
To languish in the half-broken field
Eaten with the cold fires of rust.

We remembered the black wings
And broke their congregations.

Though late, we sharpened our sickles,
And had a cave
To store a jar of wild honey for the poor.

Therefore, this winter midnight,
We will rejoice in The Bread.

1989

The Kirk in Orphir

The remains of the Round Church stand in the Orphir Kirkyard.
It was reputedly built by Earl Hakon, slayer of St Magnus,
following his penitential visit to Jerusalem.

Winter in Scapa. Five seamen
Hauled the boat high. The skipper
   Wrung salt and snow
   From his russet beard.

They stood, wrapped, on the Orphir shore.
The skipper considered the stories –
   The burning forts,
   A battle on the ice,

Churches in the Celtic west
Cleared of chalice and candlesticks,
   Chant and saga
   In red blood scrawled . . .

Stars pierced them like nails.
In the Round Kirk, candles,
   A bell, boys' mouths:
   Gloria in excelsis . . .

September 1986

Travellers

After the rockpools, beyond the cliff of Rowe
Nothing but moor, the wind too sharp
   To light sticks under the kettle,

Far less stew this rabbit. Sunset
With sleet covered the hasty tent.
   Too cold for sleep that night.

Mile after mile, bog, and the donkey
Trudged, rattling with cans.
   At Yesnaby, in a green hollow,

We put crabs in the kettle, and sang
And were sleepy, but couldn't wait,
   The waves pealing from west

At the caverned crags, and we had
A hundred Hamnavoe doors to knock on.
   Stars lit us over the Black Crag,

Lamps in farmhouse windows then
Till we came to the bell and candles at Warbeth.
   There, at midnight, we knelt.

September 1986

113

Three Sons

Five cod from the west. The boy
　　Beaches the boat, brings
The bunched fish up to the bothy.
　　The mother guts, cleans,
Lays the silver in salt, in smoke.

A lantern in the barn. A boy
　　Threshes two sheaves, oats
Spatter the floor, a golden rain.
　　Then winnowing, millstones,
The mother with crusted loaves.

Skull-food, swine-husk, till The Word
　　Drew chaos to a dance
Of shepherds, angels, kings,
　　Plough and net in a chapel
The Word, the Star-child, Mary.

1995

114

Hamnavoe Women and the Warbeth Bell: Midwinter

One said, 'I thought I heard on the stone a midnight
    keel.'
(It was the Yuletide bell.)

One said, 'So cold! I heard the chain of ice in the burn.'
(The bell unleashed its tongue, *Christ is born*.)

One said, 'A bairn, surely, a cry at the sea wall.'
(Through their salt sleep the bronze echoes fell.)

One said, 'A wave broke, white on black, far out, on the
    Breckness Rock.'
(The bronze reeled and brimmed with another stroke.)

One said, 'I dreamed an angel stood in our door.'
(Brightness on brightness unfurled through the bleak air.)

One said, 'Five fish on my hungry doorstep I found.'
(There are waverings deeper than sound.)

One said, 'I baked two sun-cakes on my hearth.'
(*Gloria*, cried the bell to the village and all the earth.)

November 1987

115

Christmas

'Toll requiem', said sun to earth,
As the grass got thin.
The star-wheel went, all nails and thorns,
Over mill and kirk and inn.

The old sun died. The widowed earth
Tolled a black bell.
'Our King will return,' said root to bone,
To the skeleton tree on the hill.

At midnight, an ox and an ass,
Between lantern and star
Cried, *Gloria . . . Lux in tenebris . . .*
In a wintered byre.

1994

Epiphany: The Shepherd

'No,' said Jock and Howie and Jimmag in 'The Selkie',
'There'll be no snow.'
The two fishermen said nothing. There will be snow.

Last year six sheep disappeared
In the gray drifts.
We dug four out, dazzled with blue and gold.

Two months till the lambing. Sometimes
I go down to 'The Selkie'.
We play dominoes, between the lamp and the fire.

Yesterday, a bar of pale gold on the floor,
The climbing sun. No wind.
But incense of ice at sunset.

Trek of a funeral past my door, the hill croft
Estquoy shuttered.
Eight wraiths in a first flurry of flakes.

'Foolish flock,' I say to the queen ewe, Flossie.
'Huddle them under the lee hill.
I can't see every fleece in a blizzard like this.'

No snow to speak of this winter, though.
A tinker
Supped a bowl of porridge at the table.

A man came by with a map.
I didn't know the ruin he was looking for.
A sailor, I think.

There was another stranger. He thanked me
Under the first star.
Those three came just before the big snow.

9 January 1992

The Three Kings

This Epiphany carol was set to music by the American folk singer, Pete Seeger.

They're looking for what, the three kings,
Beyond their border?
A new Kingdom, peace and truth and love,
Justice and order.

One was black and one was brown
And one was yellow.
A star crooked its jewelled finger.
The three kings follow.

How did they fare, the three kings?
Where did they dine?
They lived on a crust or two
And sour wine.

One was yellow and one was black
And one was brown.
They passed a scorched and rutted plain
And a broken town.

Whom did they meet, the three kings,
Among the thorns?
Herod's captains hunting
With dogs and horns.

119

One was brown and one was yellow
And one was black.
Here's what they found, a refugee bairn
Wrapped in a sack.

What did they do, the three kings,
When they got home?
In Vietnam, Rhodesia, Kashmir, troubled they bide
Till the Kingdom come.

Christmas 1966

An Old Woman in Winter

Snow blossomed,
Snow withered and shrank the heart.
One year an old man at the fire
Nodded upon silence.
I remember a child
And a apple
And many stars outside,
A first cradle-load.
The tree was green.
The tree was tall.
The tree was broken into lights.
There was a winter
Of no trees,
But soldiers stayed in this house and that.
Even the king,
It was said, lacked
And was moved from town to town.
I know, most winters
The rich children got silver dolls and birds
And a poor child
Clapped hands over a coloured stone.
Plenty of stars and beggars always.
In the year of the soldiers
There was no beggar,
All held out hands, mute, like bare twigs.
When I was a child
The snow was higher than me
And bell-cry and bird and candle

Brighter than snow.
Life, a cartload of days, at last, thankfully
Draws to winter,
To silence and to darkness.
For new breath, soon,
The snow, the bells, anguish, the birds and the gifts.

18 December 1976

Druim Chinoiseries

FOURTEEN DRUIM CHINOISERIES
(POEMS FROM THE CHINESE)

Druim House is in Nairn. Pluscarden Abbey is in Elgin. Macbeth met the three witches near Forres.

1

Rain falls and falls.
A beautiful horse grazes in the meadow,
How high, the lime tree!
The house is full of friends and laughter.

2

The starlings in the chimney,
So far
They haven't dropped into my room
To waken me with matins.
There was one bluebottle.
Alas! he is lying legs-up under the mirror.

3

I hear more guests arriving.
They are all sitting
Round a log fire, laughing.
Soon
I must go out and join the wedding guests.
This is selfishness,
Writing poems alone before a mirror.

The monks are chanting
Their office at Pluscarden.
Between here and there
King Macbeth met the witches.
An Orkney earl
Went to meet the Scottish king fearfully.
I think of the monks
With the light of storied glass
On praising mouths.

If the sun comes out
I will walk through the beautiful garden.
When it rains outside
It is perhaps better
To drink wine with friends round a log fire.

Yesterday the trees were like ghosts.
Today the Black Isle is a blur.
In Orkney
Does the sun shine? More likely
A storm is prowling among the hills and firths.

Lovely the yellow lanterns of laburnum.
Lovely the great rich clusters of rhododendrons.
I didn't know
The lime tree would be so kind to us.
Last night, late,
We drank tea from French lime-blossom.

How pleasant, to eat Shetland salmon with friends
And talk about poetry.
I saw a beautiful cat two days ago,
Then it flowed up the stairs.
I have not seen it again.
I must tell my black cat Gypsy all about this.

The sun is driving gray flocks
To water the earth.
Trees and grass are glad of the rain.
Tomorrow, they know
The sun will throw a golden coat over them.
Today the wind is at home.

What more could I ask for?
A little white room
A bed, a chair, a lamp.
I sit at the window
Writing verses on small white squares of Pluscarden paper.

There's a wild sweet blackbird.
He sings and sings
Between a leafy branch and broken crystals of cloud.

In the mirror in the window
I see
A thousand gray hairs.

Don't look any more!
Quick, write a new verse
Before another black hair turns to ash.

13

Where are the two big dogs?
They wrestle
Boisterously and merrily.
Nuff the black dog
Is like a cloud to them
With an occasional rumble of thunder in his throat.
As we break biscuits
They crack open huge bones.

14

Lilac and juniper and lime
Talk to me
More convincingly than politicians
Who are husting
Today, in the rain,
The beautiful Arab horse, El Callil,
Crossed the field to us.
Then we had to turn our faces
To the mountains and firths.

June 1987

Three Songs of Success (in a Chinese style)

1

This is bitterness.
Knowledgeable men are praising you for a thing
    accomplished
(Except for an envious one
And another you have unknowingly hurt),
To have to turn away from the wine-glasses at last
And live with the lonely certainty of failure.

2

This is bitterness too –
To have burned much oil
And broken many pens,
To make a precious thing for a friend:
Then to have her flick a page,
And give her passing beauty back to the sun.

3

There is a third bitterness –
To put more and more of one's joy,
As the flesh shrivels,
On a white page with black markings on it,
So that the young
May learn the various categories of joy.

2 June 1972

The Friend

Stone, tree, star, fish, animal, man,
All gathered
Within one circle of light and fire.
And think in Orkney
Of the old friendship of stone and man,
How they honoured and served each other,
The fire on the hearth, blue tremblings
Of water in well and wall-niche,
The stone bed,
The stones that children enchant on the shore
To ship or castle,
Querns that ground corn,
The Book of the Dead –
Stone pages, celebrations in the kirkyard.

6 April 1985

The Elemental Stone

'I am blessed by stone and the water in the hollow stone. Light beats about the stone. The stone has come from the fire at the heart of earth.'

Here, offered, over and over, the stone of our beginning and end.

The bride: 'I have taken a white rose from his hand' . . . (And air and fire and snow laboured and danced also at the forging of root and petal.)

Ploughman and plough unlocked the stone. 'The stone stands tall in sun and wind and rain, stone broken into cornstalks, multitudes.'

The fisherman holds a course clear of reef and crag. 'I will come soon to the well-built stone pier – wind in the sail – with the bounty of salt and water.' (The quarry, beyond, is a broken wave of fossils.)

The gravedigger turns his key. Sun and air and water of grief have fallen briefly on the dead. And, 'This stone will be carved with a new good name,' he says.

And the monk, 'Here we will build arch upon arch, stone fountains. A candle will burn and shine in a niche. There will be water of blessing in a worn eight-sided font. The air between red pillars will move, night and morning, with the ordered cry of our mouths.'

February 1988

The Solstice Stone

'All were locked in me,
  Silence and darkness.
  I was a thing of winter.
  Hollowed, I might lodge a skull.
  I was barrenness.
  I was the block rejected by mason, carver,
    shaper of querns.'

A star unlocked the stone.
  The stone was a white rose.
  It was a dove.
  It was a harp with a hundred carols.
  It was a cornstalk.
  It was the candle at sunset.
  It was a fountain, cluster of arches.

On that stone lie the loaves and the cup.

October 1987

Waters

'All the rivers run into the sea' –
From high Grampian gleams,
From dawn-dew, springs in rocks,
Atlantic clouds
Plucking harps in the Gaelic west,
From stone throats in ancient rose-gardens,
From burn and loch where trout
Make insect circles at sunset,
From juices of buried creatures
Purified in the deep cells of clay,
From the eye brightness
That seeped upon a stone through the small knuckles of
    Inga
After her blackbird died –
All gathered earth lucency
Seeps on and out
To the seven bitternesses of ocean:

That the ships may cross
Freighted with corn and guns and voyagers.

c. *1985*

A Dream of Christmas

In his garden, under white roses, an old man
Confused by the seasons, cried –

   'For my last Christmas, a dance of children only.
   One will be masked as a snowflake,
   One as a star,
   One as the red-beaded holly,
   One as a dove,
   One as an ox housed from sun and furrows,
   One as a surging-crested-breaking wave
   – Masks of all natural things
   I bid to the feast,
   All but the mask of ore, that has withered
   History to the root
   And wintered me, hearthstone and heart.'

Time opened. It covered the sleeper
In whitest drifts.
   At the garden gate
A black boy stood with a golden apple.

October 1986

Uranium 1

*This and the following poem were written at the height of the
controversy arising from a proposal by the nuclear industry to
make test drillings in the West Mainland of Orkney.*

We passed through the Door of Stone.
We stayed a while, with tusks and ashes.
We left.
The stones fell, silently.

The Door of Bronze opened to us.
In the square
Masques were danced: battle, harvest, hunt.
Time dimmed those pillars.
The streets lay empty.
The tribe had moved far on.

Always the Door of Salt
Had stood open.
We entered, returned with fish.
Quick thrustings, takings:
Always a few did not return.

The Green Door –
A man forged a key to that,
After fire, brimmings of iron music.
The barns lie fair to the sun.
Here
We have broken bread a winter or two.

This, we are assured,
Is not the place still
Where the tribe
Will write history on skins
And seal it in a jar, cave-kept.
A horseman
Returned across the desert this morning.
On the far side
He had stood before a door that had no name.

May 1978

Uranium 2

A fist beat on a winter stone.
Let the sun in!
Wind and rain and sun, let them in!

The stone opened.
Plough and ox went in at the door of stone.
Stone and seed mixed pure grainings.
That was the House of Corn.
The sun burned on the hearth.
A man, a woman, a child broke bread (the sun) at a board.
This dance of earth, air, water, fire
(Though threatened always
By soldier and rat and worm),
This has circled
For six thousand summers, a green dance.

The great sun-key,
The plough,
Lies in the barn
Till the green word is uttered, each spring.
The earth door opens.
The ceremony of bread begins again.

*

A stranger
Knocks today at the ancient door.
(He does not smell of roots or rain,

He smells of nothing.
His face is a blank mask.
$E=mc^2$ is the mark on his key.)
Under your furrows, islanders,
A treasure richer than cornstalks.
At the hearth, grandmother and child.
There was once a dragon and it came to the king's gate.
Shall we barter dove and the ear of corn
For dragon eggs?
Shall we open the door? What story, the old or the new?
We have lived so long and so well
In our green fable.
Shall we open the doors?

1979

Bird and Island

A bird visited an island,
Lodged in a cliff,
A stone web of mathematics and music.

Bird whirled, built, brooded on
Three blue eggs.

A bird visited the island,
Sun by sun, aloof
From wild pig and dolphin and fossil
But woven into
The same green and blue.

The bird returned to the island,
Saw curves of boat and millstone,
Suffered fowler and rock-reft.

The bird, sun-summoned,
Turned slow above
The harp, the fire, the axe.

Bird and boy
Shared crust and crab.

Bird brooded
On a million breaking rock songs.

Bird visited, hesitant,
The island of wheels.

Bird entered
The heavy prisms of oil.

Flame now, bird, in your nest
Of broken numbers.

1976

Summer and Winter

I was happy, one afternoon in summer,
When a kind lady
Asked me to write a poem for the *National Schizophrenia
Newsletter*.

It was a day of carnival in Orkney,
All around
There was music and laughter
And children abroad in the sunshine
In coloured dresses,
Happy as flowers or the blue waves on the pier.

Life, I know, is not
All happiness like that day.
We must all
Endure dark times and onsets of winter.
No person born but has
Storms, barren branches, and darkness.

We should know that always and everywhere
The seed is under the snow,
Waiting,
And always it thrusts up, unfolding in the garden
Like this carnival throng
In the sunlight, in blown music and colour and laughter.

Each one
Has sat with curtains drawn against winter.

Each one has thought then
The bleakness and cold never-ending.

Listen to the summer music!
The sea is blue again, the grass is green.

1987

Children in Need

May this Greenland child
Be holding an orange and a loaf in her hand soon.
May this child from wars far east
Get a fish in his thin yellow hand.
Twins in a burnt African forest
In a cold wind
Look, a van has driven their way
With coats, blue and green.
I think, some sunset
A child dumb with grief
   May be given a guitar,
Then all children in need
   Dance under the stars
Till the bread-burdened sun rises.

3 August 1995

To the Tibetan Refugees

May the house be firmly founded.
And I hope there's a well,
Ever springing, near the door.
There should be a fire for cold nights
And a clear window, too,
To see the stars snapping silver fingers!
I imagine a cupboard
With bread and cheese and fruit in it,
So that a lost traveller may eat too.
A good bed, chairs, a table.
A jar with flowers and a book.
And may the angels of mountain and of snow
Bend perpetually over that good house.
(So wishes
One with a house beside a cold Northern sea.)

1983

Poem for Three Peoples

On the Balkan mountains
Sat clouds like doves.

The Adriatic shore
Washed by waves, endless harps.

On the mountain passes
Folk went with their goats and baskets of eggs.
Along the shores, nets drying,
Boats and children and seabirds.

And all blessed by sun and stars.

Suddenly along the mountain passes
Come women, weeping.
Houses and churches and barns burning, below.
Guns in the cornfields.

And on the shore boats broken
For irregulars to feed flames
In the first snow.

Cities of Croatia, Bosnia, Serbia,
May children climb
Out of your ruins into the sun

And the doves
Fly down upon their thin hands, soon.

1992

Ikey: His Will in Winter Written

I, Ikey Faa, being of whole and sound mind, (nobody
    thinks it but me),
do hereby bequeath and leave my possessions
to the following persons, heartily praying that
those beneficiaries make full use
of the same, to their own hearty good and the
good of all the world beside.

Item: the birds of the isle, hawk and swan,
   eider and blackbird and dotterel, to the
   child JOHN SWEYNSON that gave me and the birds a
   bite to eat in last winter snow, and I in the
   high winds of March gave the said John a
   kite I had made out of sticks and paper for to fly among
    the
   said birds.

Item: the fish in the tides and rips and
   races about this isle, to JOCK SINCLAIR fisherman in
    the
   said isle: that he having to return the
   fattest fish to the laird's plate and kitchen, in
   exchange for a farthing or a halfpenny:
   since also the fingers of the laird have not baited hooks,
                                nor his lady's fingers
   to my knowledge stunk with fish-guts,
   and there is no true truce and tryst-time
   as between hall and haul:

which season and compact are well
kent to the fishermen. I have had this and that cod-
  head
from John's goodwife.

Item: the flowers of the sun, from the first
  snowdrop to the last blown rose petal,
  to GERDA FLAWS, for I have not
  seen such delight in flowers in any
  house-bound creature, no, not in butterfly and
  bee; and I pray the said Gerda to
  ensure and guarantee all traffic as between
  bee and butterfly, sun and raindrop and
  the feast in the open bud. I wish for her
  a long happy butter-time and
  bannock-time and bairn-time, happy among flowers.

Item: I leave the land of this isle from the
  lowest rooted tangle in the ebb to the
  hawk over the hill to MANSIE GRAY and all others who
  changed it, in a thousand years and more,
  from a bog to a green-and-gold patchwork;
  and yet it wears Mansie Gray
  out, the land, it grinds him down and it
  grays him, bows and breaks him, to keep the big
  laird's house with nine empty echoing rooms and
  another in the city of Edinburgh; and forbye
  to stock the said dwellings
  with beef and bread and wine, silk and fiddles and
    etchings and harps.
  I have eaten croft-crusts with thankfulness from Mansie
    Gray's table.

Item: The burns and the winds to millers.

Item: Rain and sun and corn to the makers of ale.

Item: to the factor, a breath and a heartbeat and
   a breath, calculations, one at a time: as far as the last
      breath:
   such as are never noted among the ciphers and in the
      ledger in his office.

I, Ikey Faa, write this with a stick on snow and
mud in the quarry, three days before Yule,
having a hoast on me that does not
mend, and a fiercer burning in the
blood than I have known.

I have rejoiced greatly in the
elements that are soon to shake me out and away, all but
      earth – 'twixt
Yule and Hogmanay, as near as I can
guess – and I leave what is all mine and all men's and
      God's to them that
will enjoy and use it best.

As *Witness* – a sparrow (his splash in the ditch)
   a mouse (his scurry and snow mark)

                              *

(Will I manage to struggle to the ale-house
before closing time? If I do, will the thin-lipped
prevaricator that keeps the place give me the loan of a
last whisky?)

                                                    1995

Glossary

broch-stones	remains of circular fort
butter-kirn	churn
cheepered	cheeped
cuithes	older coal-fish
doucely	soberly, peaceably
dromond	swift medieval warship
eld	old age
enthirling	binding, enslaving
forbye	in addition
glebe	land belonging to church or earl
gowping	gaping
grave-stoor	dust from a grave
grieve	farm overseer
hirpling	limping
hoast	persistent cough
howk	dig up
kent	known
kist	chest
lowsing-time	end of working day
mercat	market
noust	sheltered inlet for boats
Orkahowe	Viking name for Maeshowe
poke	paper bag
rune	story
scooner	large beer glass
sea-haar	cold sea mist
shebeen	illicit pub
sillock	young coal-fish

skerry	*reef*
skirled	*screamed*
thwart	*rower's bench*
tilth	*soil*
Usque	*whisky*
vennels	*lanes*
whitemaa	*seagull*